UP A TREE

# Tree Kangaroos

Willow Clark

**PowerKiDS** press™

New York

Published in 2012 by The Rosen Publishing Group, Inc.
29 East 21st Street, New York, NY 10010

First Edition

Editor: Joanne Randolph
Book Design: Greg Tucker
Layout Design: Kate Laczynski

Photo Credits: Cover © www.iStockphoto.com/Norbert Bieberstein; pp. 4–5, 6–7, 12–13, 18 (top, bottom) Shutterstock.com; p. 6 (left) © www.iStockphoto.com/Mark Stay; p. 7 (right) Tim Laman/Getty Images; p. 8 © Tier und Naturfotografie/SuperStock; pp. 9, 10, 16, 20, 21, 22 © www.iStockphoto.com/Craig Dingle; p. 11 © Animals Animals/SuperStock; p. 14 Comstock/Getty Images; p. 15 Zoological Society of San Diego/Getty Images; p. 17 Martin Harvey/Getty Images; p. 19 © www.iStockphoto.com/Stephen Shaw.

Library of Congress Cataloging-in-Publication Data

Clark, Willow.
 Tree kangaroos / by Willow Clark. — 1st ed.
    p. cm. — (Up a tree)
 Includes index.
 ISBN 978-1-4488-6189-7 (library binding) — ISBN 978-1-4488-6337-2 (pbk.) — ISBN 978-1-4488-6338-9 (6-pack)
 1. Tree kangaroos—Juvenile literature.  I. Title.
 QL737.M35C53 2012
 599.2'22—dc23
                           2011031648

Manufactured in the United States of America

CPSIA Compliance Information: Batch #WW12PK: For Further Information contact Rosen Publishing, New York, New York at 1-800-237-9932

# Contents

# Meet the Tree Kangaroo

When you think of kangaroos, you likely picture the large, hopping animals that are a symbol of Australia. The tree kangaroo is this kangaroo's arboreal relative. An arboreal animal is an animal that spends most of its time in trees.

Tree kangaroos are active in both the day and night. Some kinds of tree kangaroos seem to be more active at night, though.

The tree kangaroo belongs to the macropod family. "Macropod" comes from the Greek word for "big feet." Tree kangaroos are also **marsupials**. A marsupial is a **mammal** that has a pouch. This book will introduce you to this curious animal and its life up in the trees.

# Up in the Cloud Forest

## Where Tree Kangaroos Live

New Guinea

Indian
Ocean

AUSTRALIA

Queensland

Pacific
Ocean

**MAP KEY**

Tree kangaroo range

Tree kangaroos live in the Australian state of Queensland and on the island of New Guinea. They live in rain forests and cloud forests. A cloud forest is a rain forest in a mountainous place. It gets its name because it is often foggy or cloudy within the tree **canopies**.

Top: This Goodfellow's tree kangaroo makes its home in the tropical rain forest of the Foja Mountains, in New Guinea. *Below*: Cloud forests are forests high up on mountainsides.

The climate in the tree kangaroo's **habitat** can be warm and wet to **temperate**. Its thick fur keeps it comfortable in different kinds of weather. Its fur even sheds rain that falls on its neck and back!

# The Tree Kangaroo's Body

There are about 12 species, or kinds, of tree kangaroos. They are thickly built. Adults are between 2 and 3 feet (61–91 cm) long. The tree kangaroo's tail is about the same length as its body. Tree kangaroos

Unlike their ground-dwelling kangaroo relatives, which have large, strong back legs, tree kangaroos' front and back limbs are about the same length.

weigh between 15 and 30 pounds (7–14 kg), depending on the species.

Here you can see how long the tree kangaroo's tail is. It is used to help the animal balance, but it cannot grip things the way some arboreal animals' tails can.

The tree kangaroo's fur can be grayish, brown, or reddish brown, with yellow or cream on the belly or face. Some species have black fur on their ears or a stripe of black fur down their backs.

# Built for Branches

The tree kangaroo's claws are sharp and curved. This makes them perfect for grabbing on to tree branches.

Tree kangaroos climb trees by jumping up about 3 feet (91 cm) and wrapping their front limbs around the trunk. They then climb up to a branch. They can also hop between branches or other trees without slipping or falling.

Tree kangaroos have some special body parts that make them well **adapted** to climbing. Their front limbs are strong to help them pull themselves up the trunk. Long, curved claws on their feet help them hang on to branches. Rough pads on their feet keep them from slipping, too. The tree kangaroo's long tail helps it keep its balance as it moves through trees.

The tree kangaroo is not as fast or as graceful on the ground as it is in the trees. There, it holds its tail off of the ground and moves by taking small hops.

# Tree Kangaroo Fun Facts

**1**

Tree kangaroos do not sweat. To cool down, they wet the fur on their forearms by licking it.

**7**

Tree kangaroos live for about 10 years in the wild. In zoos, they have lived for as long as 20 years.

**2**

Only the female tree kangaroo has a pouch.

**3**

Tree kangaroos can leap to the ground from up to 60 feet (18 m) in a tree without getting hurt.

**4**

The tree kangaroo mother cleans and grooms her baby while it is in her pouch. She can fit her whole head in her pouch to reach the baby!

**5**

Tree kangaroos spend about 14 hours each day sleeping.

**6**

Many zoos feed their tree kangaroos tea leaves. These leaves have a **substance** that gives the animal its reddish-brown color. This substance is also found in leaves that tree kangaroos eat in their habitat.

**8**

In zoos, one of the tree kangaroo's favorite treats is hard-boiled eggs.

**9**

Tree kangaroo mothers usually have only one baby at a time. It is rare for them to have twins.

**10**

A female kangaroo is called a doe. A male kangaroo is called a buck.

# A Solitary Animal

All tree kangaroo species are believed to be solitary. That means they do not live in groups. Adults come together when it is time to **mate** but do not stay together. The only strong bond seems to be between a tree kangaroo mother and her offspring.

Tree kangaroos, like other solitary animals, may live alone to make sure they have enough food to eat.

If you see two tree kangaroos together, you are probably looking at a mother and her baby.

Each tree kangaroo has its own **territory** that is centered around a few large trees. Males have territories of about 11 acres (4 ha), while females have territories of about 4.5 acres (2 ha). Each male's territory overlaps with those of a few females. Females' territories do not overlap, though.

# Time to Eat!

Tree kangaroos are **omnivores**. This means that they eat both plants and animals. Most of their diet is made up of leaves. They also eat fruit, flowers, bark, tree sap, bugs, eggs, and young birds. Tree kangaroos eat throughout the day, feeding for about 20 minutes every 4 hours.

Tree kangaroos eat lots of leaves, as this Goodfellow's tree kangaroo is doing. Goodfellow's tree kangaroos like silkwood leaves the best.

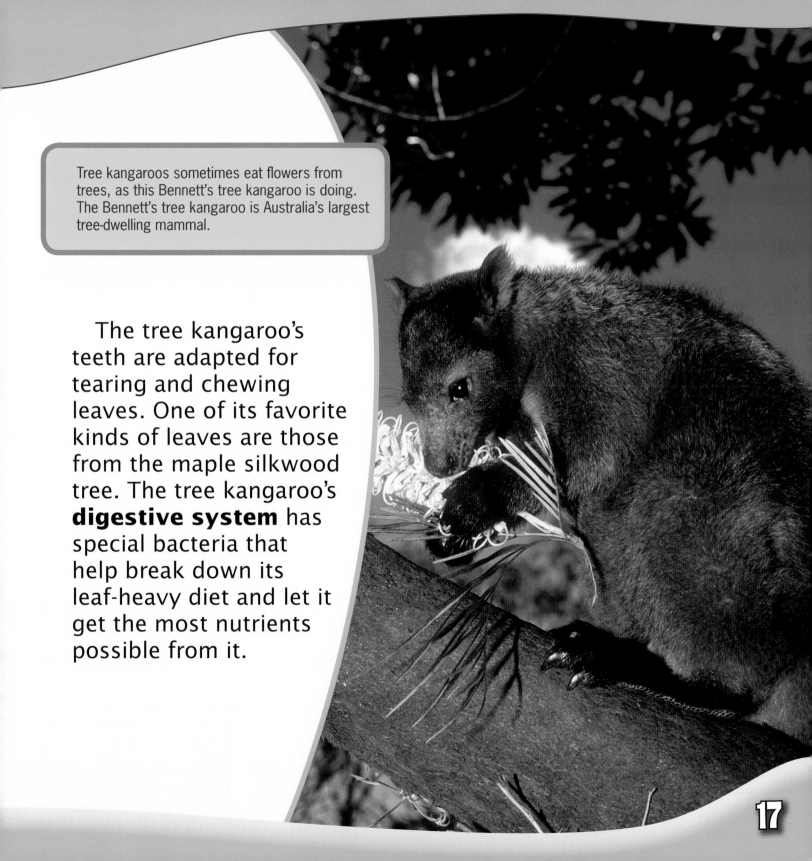

Tree kangaroos sometimes eat flowers from trees, as this Bennett's tree kangaroo is doing. The Bennett's tree kangaroo is Australia's largest tree-dwelling mammal.

The tree kangaroo's teeth are adapted for tearing and chewing leaves. One of its favorite kinds of leaves are those from the maple silkwood tree. The tree kangaroo's **digestive system** has special bacteria that help break down its leaf-heavy diet and let it get the most nutrients possible from it.

# Staying Safe

The tree kangaroo's most common **predator** is people. People hunt the tree kangaroo for its meat and skin. Tree kangaroos are also hit and killed by cars and killed by dogs. Owls, eagles, and pythons hunt tree kangaroos, too.

*Left*: Pythons are one of the dangers tree kangaroos face in the trees. *Below*: On the ground, tree kangaroos must watch out for dingoes and dogs.

If a predator finds a tree kangaroo, the tree kangaroo can try to get away by leaping to another tree or on to the ground.

The tree kangaroo's main **defense** is being out of reach of its predators. Tree kangaroos are much more easily caught when they are on the ground because they are clumsier and slower than when they are climbing. The best way for them to stay safe is by sitting among the leaves, out of sight and away from predators on the ground.

# Joeys

Tree kangaroo babies start to peek out of the pouch at around eight months old.

Tree kangaroos mate throughout the year. The baby, or joey, is born about 45 days after mating and crawls into the mother's pouch. The joey is less than 1 inch (2.5 cm) long and hairless. The newborn joey stays in its mother's pouch and drinks her milk while it develops.

> A tree kangaroo mother and baby stay together for about one and a half years.

At about 10 months old, the joey leaves the pouch for the first time. It stops drinking its mother's milk at about 13 months old. It is now ready to eat an adult diet. When it is about 18 months old, the young tree kangaroo leaves its mother to live on its own.

# Tree Kangaroos in Danger

Seven of the twelve species of tree kangaroos are **endangered**. Besides being hunted by people, the biggest threat to tree kangaroos is habitat loss. Many of the forests where tree kangaroos live have been cut down for lumber or for coffee, rice, or wheat farms. Habitat loss leaves tree kangaroos with fewer places to live.

Tree kangaroos are interesting animals, and they are an important part of their rain forest habitats.

Groups like the World Wildlife Fund are working to save tree kangaroos and their habitat. They teach people about the effects of hunting and habitat loss. They are working hard to save the tree kangaroo from becoming **extinct**.

# Glossary

**adapted** (uh-DAPT-ed)  Changed to fit new conditions.

**canopies** (KA-nuh-peez)  The tallest trees or branches in rain forests.

**defense** (dih-FENTS)  Something a living thing does that helps keep it safe.

**digestive system** (dy-JES-tiv SIS-tem)  The body parts that help turn the food an animal eats into the power its body needs.

**endangered** (in-DAYN-jerd)  In danger of no longer existing.

**extinct** (ik-STINGKT)  No longer existing.

**habitat** (HA-buh-tat)  The kind of land where an animal or a plant naturally lives.

**mammal** (MA-mul)  A warm-blooded animal that has a backbone and hair, breathes air, and feeds milk to its young.

**marsupials** (mahr-SOO-pee-ulz)  Animals that carry their young in pouches.

**mate** (MAYT)  To come together to make babies.

**omnivores** (OM-nih-vawrz)  Animals that eat both plants and animals.

**predator** (PREH-duh-ter)  An animal that kills other animals for food.

**substance** (SUB-stans)  Any matter that takes up space.

**temperate** (TEM-puh-rut)  Not too hot or too cold.

**territory** (TER-uh-tor-ee)  Land or space that animals guard for their use.

# Index

# Web Sites

Due to the changing nature of Internet links, PowerKids Press has developed an online list of Web sites related to the subject of this book. This site is updated regularly. Please use this link to access the list:
www.powerkidslinks.com/uptr/kanga/